Curries
& Kadhis

TARLA DALAL

India's # 1 Cookery Author

S&C

SANJAY & CO.

MUMBAI

First Printing : 2005

Copyright © Sanjay & Co.

ISBN : 81-89491-11-3

Price: Rs. 89/-

Published & Distributed by : **Sanjay & Company**

353/A-1, Shah & Nahar Industrial Estate, Dhanraj Mill Compound, Lower Parel (W), Mumbai - 400 013. INDIA.

Tel. : (91-22) 2496 8068 ● Fax : (91-22) 2496 5876 ● E-mail : sanjay@tarladalal.com

Printed by : **Jupiter Prints**, Mumbai

Recipe Research & Production Design	**Nutritionists**	**Photography**	**Designed by**
Arati Fedane	Nisha Katira	Jignesh Jhaveri	Satyamangal Rege
Umaima Abdulally	Sapna Thakkar		
	Food Styling	**Typesetting**	
	Shubhangi Dhaimade	Adityas Enterprises	

DISCLAIMER

While every precaution has been taken in the preparation of this book, the publishers and the author assume no responsibility for errors or omissions. Neither is any liability assumed for damages resulting from the use of information contained herein. And of course, no book is a substitute for a qualified medical advice. So it is wiser to modify your dietary patterns under the supervision of a doctor or a nutritionist.

BULK PURCHASES

Tarla Dalal Cookbooks are ideal gifts. If you are interested in buying more than 500 assorted copies of Tarla Dalal Cookbooks at special prices, please contact us at 91-22-2496 8068 or email : sanjay@tarladalal.com

❦ INTRODUCTION ❧

Dear Friends,

We get umpteen letters from harassed homemakers who want help deciding what gravy-based dishes go best not only with *chapattis, parathas* or *rotis,* but also with rice. I have to admit it can be a daunting task to think up appealing meals every day that will please not only your fussy family, but also satisfy your creative urges!

This common dilemma was the inspiration behind Curries & Kadhis, which consists of 41 recipes for regular as well as innovative accompaniments for both *rotis* and rice. In addition to all time favourites like *Methi Mutter Malai, Subz Makhni* and *Mirchi ka Salan* are also other easy to make recipes like *Dahi Bhindi* and *Quick Potato Curry.* Among the *kadhi* recipes are some popular ones from different parts of the country, such as *Punjabi Kadhi, Sindhi Kadhi* and *Gatte ki Kadhi.* Wholesome and appetising, they are guaranteed to add interest to your table.

I have also featured some well-known international curries like Thai Red Curry, Vietnamese Curry, and Ceylonese Curry, for those days when you want to serve up a flamboyant foreign meal.

So wipe that stressed-out look off your face and start experimenting with style! Your family is going to love these exciting additions to the menu.

Regards,

Tarla Dalal

❧ CONTENTS ❧

CURRIES

INTERNATIONAL CURRIES

KADHIS

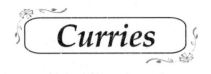

Curries

~ Nawabi Curry ~

Truly, a curry with very royal taste. The key to making this curry perfectly lies in frying the paste patiently on a medium flame while stirring continuously till the mixture leaves oil

Preparation time: 30 minutes.   Cooking time: 20 minutes.   Serves 4.

1 cup boiled mixed vegetables (cauliflower, carrot, french beans, peas)
1½ cups chopped tomatoes
a few strands of saffron *(kesar)*, optional
1 tsp sugar
4 tbsp oil
Salt to taste

For the paste

¾ cup sliced onions
1 tbsp broken cashewnuts *(kaju)*
1 tbsp chopped almonds *(badam)*
2 tsp coriander *(dhania)* seeds
2 tsp cumin *(jeera)* seeds
1 tbsp poppy seeds *(khus-khus)*
2 tsp aniseeds *(vilayati saunf)*
2 tbsp freshly grated coconut
2 tsp chopped ginger
1 tsp chopped green chillies
4 whole dry red chillies, broken into pieces
1 to 2 cardamoms *(elaichi)*
2 cloves *(laung)*
25 mm. (1") piece cinnamon *(dalchini)*
7 curry leaves *(kadi patta)*

For the paste
Grind to a smooth paste adding a little water. Keep aside.

How to proceed

1. Add 1½ cups of water to the tomatoes and boil for 10 to 12 minutes. When soft, cool and prepare a purée by blending in a blender and straining the mixture through a sieve. Keep aside.
2. Heat the oil in a pan and sauté the ground paste for 4 to 5 minutes, till it starts leaving oil from the sides.
3. Add the tomato purée, sugar and salt.
4. Warm the saffron in a small vessel, add a little milk (approximately 1 tablespoon), rub in until the saffron dissolves and add to the curry.
5. Add the boiled vegetables and bring it to a boil. Serve hot.

~ Malai Kofta ~

An extra special party favourite. Melt in the mouth koftas are the highlight of this curry. Use only the freshest paneer to ensure good results

Preparation time: 25 minutes.   Cooking time: 30 minutes.   Serves 4.

For the koftas
1½ cups *paneer* (cottage cheese)
3 tbsp plain flour *(maida)*
1 tsp baking powder
½ tbsp finely chopped green chillies
1 tbsp chopped coriander
Salt to taste
Oil for deep frying

For the gravy
3 cups chopped tomatoes
½ cup fresh cream
1 tsp chilli powder

4 tbsp oil
Salt to taste

To be ground into a paste with a little water
¾ cup sliced onions
2 tbsp freshly grated coconut
4 cloves garlic
1 tsp chopped green chillies
2 whole dry red chillies
2 tsp coriander *(dhania)* seeds
1 tsp cumin seeds *(jeera)*
2 tbsp piyal seeds *(charoli)*
2 tsp poppy seeds *(khus-khus)*
1 tsp grated ginger
2 tsp chopped fresh coriander

For the koftas
1. Crumble the *paneer* and mix the plain flour, baking powder, green chillies, coriander and salt.
2. Knead well till smooth.

3. Shape into small balls and deep fry in hot oil till golden brown in colour. Fry two koftas at a time otherwise they separate. Keep the koftas aside.

For the gravy
1. Add 3 cups of water to the tomatoes and cook them. When soft, prepare a purée by blending in a blender and then passing through a sieve.
2. Heat the oil in a vessel and fry the paste very well.
3. Add the chilli powder and fry again for 1 minute.
4. Add the tomato purée and salt and boil the gravy for at least 10 to 15 minutes.
5. Add in the cream, mix and switch off the gas.

How to proceed
Just before serving, heat the gravy and add the koftas.
Serve hot with parathas, puris or rice.

Handy tip : You can add 1 cup of boiled green peas to the gravy if you like.

Methi Mutter Malai

A tasty combination of fenugreek leaves and green peas. If you like a slight bitter taste of the methi in your curry reduce the soaking time at step 1 to 5 minutes

Preparation time: 20 minutes.   Cooking time: 15 minutes.   Serves 4.

3 cups chopped fenugreek *(methi)* leaves
½ tsp cumin seeds *(jeera)*
½ cup chopped onion
2 large tomatoes
1 cup boiled green peas
1 cup milk
A pinch sugar
3 tbsp oil
Salt to taste

To be ground into a paste
¾ cup sliced onions
1 tbsp chopped green chillies

25 mm. (1") piece ginger
3 cloves garlic
2 tbsp broken cashewnuts *(kaju)*
2 tsp poppy seeds *(khus-khus)*

For the dry masala (to be roasted lightly and powdered)
2 small sticks cinnamon *(dalchini)*
4 cloves *(laung)*
2 cardamoms *(elaichi)*
3 peppercorns
1 tsp cumin seeds *(jeera)*

14

1. Wash the fenugreek leaves and soak in water with ½ teaspoon salt. Wait for 15 minutes and then squeeze out the water.
2. Put the tomatoes in hot water for 10 minutes. Remove and blend into a smooth purée in the blender.
3. Heat 2 tablespoons of oil, add the cumin seeds and fry until they crackle. Add the fenugreek leaves and cook stirring continuously for 3 to 4 minutes. Remove the fenugreek leaves and keep aside.
4. Add the remaining 1 tablespoon of oil and heat again. Add the onion and fry until golden.
5. Add the paste and fry for 1 minute till paste leaves oil from the sides. Add the tomato purée and dry masala and fry again. Add the peas, fenugreek, milk, sugar, salt and a little water and cook for a few minutes.
Serve hot.

Paneer Palak

Even before you taste it the look tempts you. To retain the bright green appearance,
add the spinach purée only when you are ready to serve.
Reheating will turn it blackish

Preparation time: 10 minutes.   Cooking time: 20 minutes.   Serves 4.

1 cup *paneer* (cottage cheese), cut into 12 mm. (½") cubes
5 cups spinach *(palak)* leaves
½ cup finely chopped onions
2 cloves garlic
12 mm. (½") piece grated ginger
2 tsp chopped green chillies
½ cup tomato purée
¼ tsp *garam masala*
2 tbsp oil
Salt to taste
Oil for deep frying

1. Boil enough water with salt and blanch spinach in it. Drain and wash spinach in cold water. This helps retain its bright green colour.
2. Blend in a liquidiser to a smooth purée. Keep aside.
3. Heat the oil in a pan and deep fry the *paneer* for a while. Remove on absorbent paper and keep in a bowl of water. This gives the paneer velvetty texture.
4. Heat the oil in a pan and fry the onions till they turn translucent.
5. Add the garlic, ginger and green chillies and fry for some time.
6. Add the tomato purée and fry stirring continuously till the mixture leaves oil.
7. Add the spinach purée, *garam masala, paneer* and salt with ¼ cup water bring to boil.

Serve hot.

❧ Paneer Tikki Pasanda ❧

Picture on facing page.

Paneer tikkis served in a gravy rich in herbs and spices. Tandoori Paneer may be added instead of the paneer tikkis to make Paneer Tikka Pasanda

Preparation time: 25 minutes.   Cooking time: 10 minutes.   Serves 4.

For the tikkis
2 cups *paneer* (cottage cheese)
1 tbsp finely chopped green chillies
¼ cup plain flour *(maida)*
Salt to taste
Oil for cooking

For the paste no.1
1 cup roughly chopped onion
4 cloves garlic
12 mm. (½") piece ginger
2 tbsp broken cashewnuts *(kaju)*

PANEER TIKKI PASANDA : Recipe above. ➙

For the paste no.2
1 cup sliced onions

Other ingredients
1 cup beaten fresh curds *(dahi)*
½ tsp *garam masala*
1 tsp chilli powder
2 tbsp oil
Salt to taste
Oil for deep frying

For the tikkis
1. Mash the *paneer* well.
2. Add the green chillies, plain flour and salt and mix well.
3. Shape into tikkis and cook on a non-stick tava by adding a little oil from the sides while cooking.

For the paste no. 1
1. Boil the onions in 1 cup of water until soft.
2. Add the garlic, ginger and cashewnuts and blend in a mixer to make a smooth paste.

For the paste no. 2
Deep fry the onions in oil until golden and make a paste in a grinder using little water.

How to proceed
1. Heat the oil in a vessel. Add the paste no. 1 and cook on a low flame for a few minutes.
2. Add the chilli powder and *garam masala*, mix and cook again, till the masala leaves oil from sides.
3. Add the beaten curds. Mix well and go on stirring all the time.
4. Cook for a while. Add the paste no.2 and salt and cook for another 5 minutes.
5. Arrange the *paneer* tikkis in a plate. Pour the hot gravy on the top. Serve hot.

Vegetable Korma

*A rich spicy vegetable. If you add nine vegetables in this recipe,
you get navratna korma*

Preparation time: 15 minutes.   Cooking time: 15 minutes.   Serves 4.

1½ cups *paneer* (cottage cheese), cut into 25 mm. (1") cubes
2 cups mixed boiled vegetables (carrots, french beans, potatotes, cauliflower), cut
into 25 mm. (1") cubes
¼ cup green peas
3 medium sized tomatoes
¾ cup chopped onions
1 tsp ginger-garlic paste
½ tsp turmeric *(haldi)* powder
2 tsp coriander *(dhania)* powder
1½ tsp chilli powder
1 tsp *garam masala*
1 cup milk
3 tbsp fresh cream

2 tbsp oil
1 tbsp butter
Salt to taste
Oil for deep frying

1. Put the tomatoes in 3 cups hot water. After 10 minutes, drain out the water, remove and peel off the skin.
2. Chop finely and keep aside.
3. Deep fry the *paneer* cubes in oil till golden brown. Drain on absorbent paper and keep aside.
4. Heat the oil and butter in vessel and fry the onions for a few minutes.
5. Add the ginger-garlic paste and fry for ½ minute.
6. Add the tomatoes, turmeric powder, coriander powder, chilli powder, *garam masala* and salt. Fry for at least 3 to 4 minutes.
7. Add the boiled vegetables peas, milk, cream and fried *paneer* pieces.
8. Cook for a few minutes.
   Serve hot with parathas.

ꙮ Malabari Curry ꙮ

Picture on page 1.

Coconut gives the dish it's distinctive aroma

Preparation time: 20 minutes.   Cooking time: 25 minutes.   Serves 4.

2 cups boiled mixed vegetables (french beans, carrots, potatoes, cauliflower, peas)
1 cup freshly grated coconut
½ cup chopped onion
2 curry leaves *(kadi patta)*
¼ tsp turmeric *(haldi)* powder
½ cup chopped tomato
½ tsp lemon juice
Salt to taste

For the paste
½ cup freshly grated coconut or 25 grams desiccated coconut
3 to 4 curry leaves *(kadi patta)*
1 tbsp cooked rice
1 tsp chopped green chillies

4 cloves garlic
1 stick cinnamon (*dalchini*)
1 cloves (*laung*)
2 nos. black peppercorns (*kali mirch*)
1 whole dry red chilli, broken into pieces

For the paste
1. Dry roast the coconut, curry leaves and rice and on a tava on a slow flame, stirring continuously, until the mixture is light pink.
2. Add the green chillies, garlic, cinnamon, cloves, peppercorns and red chilli. Remove from flame, cool and blend to a smooth paste in a blender using very little water. Keep aside.

How to proceed
1. Add 2 cups of water to the grated coconut and blend in a blender. Strain through a muslin cloth and squeeze out the coconut milk.
2. Add the paste, all the vegetables (except the tomato), onion, curry leaves and turmeric powder and cook for 15 to 20 minutes or until the vegetables are soft.
3. Add the chopped tomato and cook for 2 to 3 minutes.
4. Add the lemon juice and salt.
   Serve hot.

Subz Makhni

Try my version of this popular gravy. Umpteen variations like Paneer Makhni, Kofta Makhni etc. can be made using this gravy as the base. The gravy can also be frozen for use at a further date

Preparation time: 15 minutes.   Cooking time: 20 minutes.   Serves 4.

2 cups mixed boiled vegetables (cauliflower, french beans, carrots, peas)
½ cup cubed *paneer* (cottage cheese)
1 tsp chilli powder
2 cups fresh tomato purée
1 tsp cumin *(jeera)* powder
½ tsp *garam masala*
1 tsp *kasuri methi* (dried fenugreek leaves)
1 tbsp honey
¼ cup milk
¼ cup cream
1 tbsp oil
2 tbsp butter

Salt to taste

To be ground to a paste
1 cup chopped onions
25 mm. (1") piece ginger
4 cloves garlic
2 tbsp broken cashewnuts *(kaju)*

1. Heat the oil in a pan, add the ground paste and cook till it is light brown in colour.
2. Add the chilli powder and tomato purée and cook for a few minutes.
3. Add the cumin powder, *garam masala* and ½ cup of water and cook for some time till the oil separates from the masala. Keep aside.
4. In another pan, melt the butter, add the kasuri methi and onions and cook till the onions are lightly browned.
5. Add this to the tomato gravy, along with the boiled vegetables, honey, milk, cream, *paneer* and salt and allow it to come to a boil.
   Serve hot with rotis or parathas.

Handy tips : 1. Approximately 4 large tomatoes yield 2 cups tomato purée.
2. The paneer may be fried on a tava (griddle) before adding to the subzi.

৵ *Babycorn Paneer Jalfrazie* ৶

Baby corn cooked up in the traditional jalfrazie gravy of capsicum and onion

Preparation time: 10 minutes.   Cooking time: 15 minutes.   Serves 4.

6 nos. baby corn, cut into 4 lengthwise
1 cups *paneer* (cottage cheese), cut into 25 mm. (1") strips
¼ cup sliced spring onions whites
¼ cup sliced green capsicum
¼ cup sliced yellow capsicum
¼ cup sliced red capsicum
¼ tsp turmeric powder *(haldi)*
½ tsp chilli powder
½ tsp coriander-cumin seed *(dhania-jeera)* powder
½ cup sliced tomatoes
2 tbsp tomato purée
2 tbsp tomato ketchup
¼ cup chopped spring onions greens

2 tsp vinegar
½ tsp *garam masala*
¼ tsp sugar
2 tbsp chopped coriander
2 tbsp oil
Salt to taste

1. Heat the oil in a pan and add the spring onion whites and capsicums and sauté for 2 minutes.
2. Add the baby corn, turmeric powder, chilli powder, coriander-cumin seed powder, tomatoes, tomato purée, tomato ketchup and salt and sauté on a slow flame for 4 to 5 minutes till the baby corn is cooked.
3. Add the *paneer*, spring onion greens, vinegar, *garam masala* and sugar and toss lightly.
   Garnish with coriander and serve hot.

❧ *Aloo Mutter Moghlai* ❧

A North Indian favourite. Cook the potatoes well and you will never go wrong in it

Preparation time: 25 minutes.   Cooking time: 20 minutes.   Serves 4.

2 cups potatoes, cut into 25 mm. (1") cubes
2 cups green peas
2 cups sliced onions
½ cup chopped onions
½ tsp saffron *(kesar)*
2 tbsp fresh curds *(dahi)*
2 tbsp chopped coriander
4 tbsp oil
Salt to taste
Oil for deep frying

To be ground into a paste
2 tbsp coriander *(dhania)* seeds

25 mm. (1") piece ginger
6 cloves *(laung)*
4 green chillies

1. Heat oil in a pan and fry the sliced onions until golden brown in colour.
2. Cool and blend to a smooth paste in a blender.
3. Heat the oil in a kadai and fry the chopped onions for a little time. Add the ground paste and fry again for 3 to 4 minutes.
4. Add the potatoes, green peas and 2 cups of water. Cover and cook till the potatoes are done.
5. Add the onion paste and salt and mix well.
6. Crush the saffron and mix it in the curds. Add this mixture to the vegetable and simmer for a couple of minutes.
   Serve hot garnished with coriander.

～ Lahori Aloo ～

A potato dish with rich gravy

Preparation time: 15 minutes.   Cooking time: 25 minutes.   Serves 4.

4 cups baby potatoes (with skins)
1½ cups chopped tomatoes
2 sticks cinnamon *(dalchini)*
4 cloves *(laung)*
1 tbsp cumin seeds *(jeera)*
3 bay leaves *(tej patta)*
1 tsp aniseed *(vilayati saunf)*
¼ tsp asafoetida *(hing)*
1½ cups grated onions
1 tbsp ginger-garlic paste
1 cup milk
4 tbsp oil
Salt to taste
Oil for deep-frying

To be ground into a paste

4 whole dry Kashmiri red chillies, broken into pieces
3 tbsp coriander (*dhania*) seeds
1 tbsp cumin (*jeera*) seeds
1 tbsp poppy seeds (*khus-khus*)
1 tbsp aniseed (*vilayati saunf*)
8 peppercorns
1 small piece mace (*javantri*)
2 sticks cinnamon (*dalchini*)
2 tbsp grated dry coconut

1. Deep fry the potatoes in oil over a medium flame with the skins on till done. You may peel them before deep frying if you want.
2. Blend the tomatoes in a liquidiser.
3. Heat 4 tbsp of oil in pan and fry the cinnamon, cloves, cumin seeds, bay leaves and aniseed for a few seconds. Add the asafoetida and the onions and fry till golden.
4. Add the ginger-garlic paste and fry for a few seconds. Add the prepared paste and fry again for 3 minutes. Add salt.
5. Add the tomato purée and fry for 2 to 3 minutes.
6. Add the milk and potatoes and cook for 1 minute. Serve hot.

Avial

Picture on page 2.

Famous South Indian vegetable stew, often enjoyed at religious festivals

Preparation time: 10 minutes.   Cooking time: 10 minutes.   Serves 4.

½ cup drumsticks cut into 25 mm. (1") pieces
½ cup french beans, cut into 25 mm. (1") pieces
½ cup cauliflower florets
½ cup white pumpkin *(doodhi / lauki)*, peeled and cut into 25 mm. (1") pieces
½ cup raw banana, peeled and cut into 25 mm. (1") pieces
½ cup red pumpkin *(kaddu)*, peeled and cut into 25 mm. (1") pieces
½ cup boiled green peas
1 tsp cumin seeds *(jeera)*
2 tbsp oil
Salt to taste

To be ground to a smooth paste
¾ cup freshly grated coconut
2 green chillies

¼ tsp turmeric powder *(haldi)*
¾ cup water
1 cup beaten fresh curds *(dahi)*

1. Heat the oil in a small pan, add the cumin seeds and sauté for 2 minutes.
2. Add the drumsticks with ¼ cup of water. Cover and cook till the drumsticks are half done.
3. Add the remaining vegetables and salt and mix well. Cover and cook till the vegetables are tender.
4. Add the paste and 1 cup of water and bring to a boil. Simmer for 5 to 6 minutes and serve hot.

❧ Corn Curry ❧

Picture on facing page.

Coconut and coriander add subtlety to this delicious green curry

Preparation time: 15 minutes.   Cooking time: 10 minutes.   Serves 4.

2 cups cooked corn
1½ cups freshly grated coconut
2 tsp corn flour
2 sticks cinnamon *(dalchini)*
2 cloves *(laung)*
2 cardamoms *(elaichi)*
2 tsp lemon juice
2 tbsp oil
Salt to taste

To be ground into a paste
½ cup sliced onions
½ cup chopped coriander

CORN CURRY : Recipe above. ➜

2 green chillies
1 tbsp freshly grated coconut
3 cloves garlic
4 tsp poppy seeds *(khus-khus)*
25 mm. (1") piece ginger

1. Add 4 cups of water to the coconut and blend in a liquidiser. Strain through a muslin cloth and squeeze out coconut milk.
2. Add the corn flour and mix well and keep aside.
3. Heat the oil in a pan and fry the paste for 2 minutes.
4. Add the cinnamon, cloves and cardamoms and fry again for a while.
5. Add the lemon juice and mix well.
6. Add the corn, coconut milk and salt. Mix well and cook for a few minutes. Serve hot.

Paneer Koftas in Spinach Gravy

Soft delicious koftas in rich spinach gravy. Remember not to heat for too long as otherwise the gravy will not be as green

Preparation time: 15 minutes.   Cooking time: 30 minutes.   Serves 4.

For the paneer koftas
½ cup grated *paneer* (cottage cheese)
¼ cup boiled and grated potatoes
1 tbsp milk powder
1 tsp chilli powder
a pinch turmeric *(haldi)* powder
¼ cup grated carrots
2 tbsp finely chopped capsicum
1 tsp grated ginger
½ tsp grated garlic
1 tbsp chopped coriander
Salt to taste
Oil for deep-frying

For the spinach sauce
2 cups finely chopped spinach *(palak)*
¾ cups fresh curds *(dahi)*
½ tsp sugar
2 tbsp oil
Salt to taste

To be ground into a paste for the spinach sauce
1 tbsp freshly grated coconut
1 tbsp broken cashewnuts *(kaju)*
1 tbsp poppy seeds *(khus-khus)*
4 cloves garlic
4 green chillies
25 mm. (1") piece ginger
1 tsp aniseed *(vilayati saunf)*

For the paneer koftas
1. Combine all the ingredients except the oil and divide it into 4 equal parts.
2. Shape into balls and deep-fry them over a medium flame till they are golden brown. Drain on absorbent paper and keep aside.

For the spinach sauce
1. Boil half cup of water, add in the spinach and cook for about 15 seconds.
2. Cool and blend in blender.
3. Heat the oil in a pan and fry the paste for 3 to 4 minutes.
4. Add the curds and fry again for 1 minute.
5. Add the spinach purée, sugar and salt and boil for 3 to 4 minutes. Keep aside.

How to serve
Just before serving, add the koftas to the spinach sauce and bring to the boil.

ᦈ Mirchi ka Salan ᧕

Peanut and sesame flavoured spicy gravy from Hyderabad

Preparation time: 20 minutes.   Cooking time: 30 minutes.   Serves 6.

6 nos. long green chilies *(Bhavnagari mirchi)*
1 tsp cumin seeds *(jeera)*
½ tsp mustard seeds *(rai)*
¼ tsp fenugreek *(methi)* seeds
¼ tsp nigella *(kalonji)* seeds
6 curry leaves *(kadi patta)*
¼ tsp turmeric powder *(haldi)*
2 tsp coriander-cumin seed *(dhania-jeera)* powder
2 tsp chilli powder
1 tbsp tamarind *(imli)* pulp
2 tbsp chopped coriander
5 tbsp oil
Salt to taste

To be ground into a paste
6 cloves garlic
12 mm. (½") piece ginger
1 onion
1 tomato
3 tbsp freshly grated coconut

To be ground into a dry peanut-sesame powder
2 tbsp roasted peanuts *(shengdana)*
2 tbsp roasted sesame seeds *(til)*
1 tbsp roasted cumin seeds *(jeera)*

1. Wash and slit the green chillies. Remove the seeds and fry in hot oil until they turn whitish in colour. Remove and keep aside.
2. In the same oil, add the cumin seeds, mustard seeds, fenugreek seeds, nigella seeds and curry leaves.
3. When the seeds crackle, add the paste and cook for 2 minutes. Add the turmeric powder, coriander-cumin seed powder, chilli powder and dry peanut-sesame powder. Cook over a low flame, stirring continuously until the oil comes out from sides. This could take upto 15 minutes.
4. Add 2 cups of water and tamarind pulp and bring it to a boil.
5. Add the fried green chillies, coriander and salt and simmer until the gravy thickens.
   Serve hot.

Dahi Bhindi

Picture on back cover.

South Indian style bhindi. My personal favourite

Preparation time: 20 minutes.   Cooking time: 15 minutes.   Serves 4.

4 cups *bhindi* (lady fingers), cut into 1½" pieces
1 tsp cumin seeds *(jeera)*
1 tsp mustard seeds *(rai)*
1 tbsp *urad dal* (split black lentils)
3 whole dry red chillies, broken into pieces
5 to 6 curry leaves *(kadi patta)*
½ cup chopped onions
1 cup chopped tomatoes
1 tsp red chilli powder
½ tsp turmeric powder *(haldi)*
¼ cup fresh curds *(dahi)*
3 tbsp oil
Salt to taste

To be ground into a paste
½ cup freshly grated coconut
2 tbsp broken cashewnuts *(kaju)*

For the bhindi
1. Heat the oil in a pan and sauté the lady fingers in oil until crisp. Remove and drain on absorbent paper.
2. Heat the oil again; add the cumin seeds, mustard seeds and urad dal. When they crackle, add the red chillies and curry leaves.
3. Add the onions and sauté until it is golden in colour.
4. Add the tomatoes, chilli powder, turmeric powder, the ground paste and salt and fry until the oil comes out from the sides.
5. Add 1¼ cups of water to the curds, beat well and add it to the mixture.
6. Add the sautéed bhindi and cook for a few minutes.
   Serve hot.

Handy Tip: If you don't wish to deep fry the bhindi you can sauté it. But the bhindi won't be as crisp.

∽ Green Peas and Mushroom Curry ❧

A curry for mushroom lovers

Preparation time: 15 minutes.   Cooking time: 15 minutes.   Serves 4.

1 cup boiled green peas
1 cup sliced mushrooms
½ cup chopped onions
1 tsp chopped garlic
3 tbsp fresh cream
4 tbsp fresh curds *(dahi)*
2 tbsp oil
Salt to taste

To be ground into a paste
5 cloves *(laung)*
25 mm. (1") piece ginger
2 tbsp broken cashewnuts *(kaju)*

2 tbsp poppy seeds *(khus-khus)*
2 cardamoms *(dalchini)*
4 green chillies

1. Blanch the mushrooms in hot water for 1 minute.
2. Heat the oil in a pan and fry the onions until golden brown.
3. Add the garlic and fry for a few seconds.
4. Add the ground paste and fry for 2 to 3 minutes.
5. Add the green peas, mushrooms, cream, curds, ½ cup of water and salt and cook for 5 minutes.
   Serve hot.

Quick Potato Curry

All time favourite potato now in a quick version

Preparation time: 10 minutes.   Cooking time: 10 minutes.   Serves 4.

2 cups boiled and peeled small potaotes
2 sticks cinnamon *(dalchini)*
2 cloves *(laung)*
2 cardamoms *(elaichi)*
4 tbsp fresh cream
½ tsp sugar (optional)
2 tbsp butter
Salt to taste

For the tomato paste
1 cup chopped tomatoes
¼ cup finely chopped onions
1 tsp finely chopped ginger

1 tsp finely chopped garlic
1 tsp red chilli powder

For the tomato paste
Blend the tomatoes, onions, ginger, garlic and chilli powder with ½ cup of water into a smooth paste in a mixer.

How to proceed
1. Heat the butter in a pan and fry the cinnamon, cloves and cardamoms for a few seconds.
2. Add the tomato paste and fry for a few minutes till the oil comes out from the sides.
3. Add the potatoes, cream, sugar and salt and cook for 5 to 6 minutes.
   Serve hot.

Moong Sprouts Korma

A healthy sprout subzi in wholesome tomato based gravy

Preparation time: 15 minutes.   Cooking time: 10 minutes.   Serves 4.

2 cups moong sprouts
2 medium sized tomatoes
¾ cup grated onions
1 tsp coriander-cumin seed *(dhana-jeera)* powder
1 tsp chilli powder
½ tsp sugar
1 cup milk
2 tbsp fresh cream
3 tbsp oil
Salt to taste

To be ground into a paste
3 cloves garlic
12 mm. (½") piece ginger

2 cardamom *(elaichi)*
1 tbsp broken cashewnuts *(kaju)*
1 tbsp poppy seeds *(khus-khus)*

1. Boil the tomatoes in hot water. After 10 minutes, remove the skin and chop.
2. Heat the oil in a pan and fry the onions until they are light pink in colour. Add the paste, the coriander-cumin seed powder and chilli powder and fry for 1 minute. Add the tomatoes and fry for 3 to 4 minutes.
3. Add the moong sprouts, ¼ cup of water, sugar and salt and cook for a few minutes.
4. Add the milk and cream and cook for a few more minutes.
   Serve hot.

Hariyali Parwal

Piquant Onion stuffing and a tangy curd gravy combination to tingle your taste buds

Preparation time: 20 minutes.   Cooking time: 20 minutes.   Serves 4.

10 tender *parwals* (pointed gourd)
3 tsp fennel seeds *(saunf)*
¾ cup chopped onions
1 tsp coriander *(dhania)* powder
¼ tsp red chilli powder
¼ tsp *garam masala*
¼ tsp *amchur* (dried mango powder)
½ tsp cumin seeds *(jeera)*
2½ tbsp oil
Salt as per taste

To be made into a paste

1 cup chopped coriander
1 green chilli
25 mm. (1") piece ginger
1½ cups fresh curds (*dahi*)

1. Grind together the fennel seeds and onions to a smooth paste.
2. Heat one tbsp of oil in a pan, add fennel seeds-onion mixture and satué till onions turn golden brown.
3. Remove from fire and add coriander powder, chilli powder, *garam masala*, amchur and salt. Mix well and keep aside.
4. Peel, wash and slit the parwals lengthwise. De-seed the parwals and fill the onion mixture into the parwals. Keep aside.
5. Heat the remaining oil in a kadhai, add the cumin seeds and let them crackle.
6. Add the stuffed parwals and stir-fry them. Add salt and ¼ cup water, cover and cook on a low flame till done.
7. Add the paste and bring to a boil whilst stirring continuously.
8. Lower the flame and simmer for 2 to 3 minutes.
   Serve hot.

✎ Goanese Potato Curry ✎

Picture on facing page.

A vegetarian curry with a non vegetarian flavour. Serve with parathas or preferably with steamed rice or pao

Preparation time: 30 minutes.   Cooking time: 30 minutes.   Serves 4.

4 cups big chunks of potatoes
1 large tomato
2 tbsp oil
Salt to taste

For the paste
2 whole onions
2 tsp poppy seeds *(khus-khus)*
2 sticks cinnamon *(dalchini)*
2 cloves *(laung)*
2 peppercorns
2 tsp coriander *(dhania)* seeds

GOANESE POTATO CURRY : Recipe above. ↪

3 whole dry red chillies, broken into pieces
¾ cup freshly grated coconut
5 cloves garlic
3 tsp oil

For the paste
1. Put 1 tsp of oil in a frying pan and fry the poppy seeds, cinnamon, cloves, peppercorns, coriander seeds and red chillies for a few minutes. Keep aside.
2. Put the onions straight on the gas and roast until they become black. Peel and discard the blackened layer and slice the onions. Keep aside.
3. Put 2 teaspoons of oil in a frying pan and fry the coconut for 1 minute.
4. Mix all these ingredients and garlic and blend to a smooth paste in the blender by adding a little water if required.

How to proceed
1. Cut the tomatoes into big pieces, add 2 cups of water and cook. When soft, prepare a soup by passing through a sieve. Keep aside.
2. Heat the oil in a kadai and add the potatoes, salt and ¾ cup of water.
3. Cover with a lid and cook till the potatoes are done.
4. Add the paste, tomato soup and salt (if required) and bring to a boil. Serve hot.

Handy Tip: If you find the gravy is too sour or chilly add 2 tbsp of milk.

Chettinad Curry

The famous South Indian curry in a vegetarian version

Preparation time: 15 minutes.   Cooking time: 15 minutes.   Serves 4.

1 cup boiled peas
2 cups cauliflower florets
1 tbsp poppy seeds *(khus-khus)*
2 tbsp broken cashewnuts *(kaju)*
25 mm. (1") piece ginger
6 cloves garlic
½ cup chopped onions
3 medium tomatoes, blended
½ tsp turmeric powder *(haldi)*
½ tsp red chilli powder
4-5 curry leaves *(kadi patta)*
½ cup milk
3 tbsp oil
Salt to taste

For the chettinad masala powder

½ cup freshly grated coconut
1 tsp coriander (*dhania*) seeds
½ tsp cumin seeds (*jeera*)
1 whole dry red chillies
3 nos. cardamom (*elaichi*)
1 tsp fennel (*saunf*) seeds
2-3 peppercorns (*kali mirch*)
2-3 cloves (*laung*)
25 mm. (1") cinnamon (*dalchini*)
1 tbsp oil

1. Soak poppy seeds and cashewnuts in hot water for 5 minutes. Drain and discard the water. Keep aside.
2. Heat one tbsp of oil in a pan and roast the chettinad masala ingredients till you get a nice aroma.
3. Grind together the roasted chettinad masala, poppy seeds, cashewnuts, ginger and garlic with ¼ cup water to make a fine paste.
4. Heat two tbsp of oil in a kadhai and add the onions. Sauté till the onions turn translucent.
5. Add the pureéd tomatoes, salt, turmeric, and chilli powder.

6. Cook till the tomatoes are well blended with the masala and oil separates from the sides.
7. Add the ground paste and curry leaves and sauté for 2 minutes.
8. Add 3 cups of water, cover and cook till the gravy thickens.
9. Add the milk, mix well and switch off the flame.
   Serve hot with steamed rice.

❧ Corn-On-The-Cob Curry ❧

'Bhuttas' now form a part of this curry

Preparation time: 10 minutes.   Cooking time: 15 minutes.   Serves 4.

2 whole corns, cut into ½" thick roundels
1½ cups chopped onions
½ cup chopped tomatoes
1 tsp red chilli powder
4 tbsp oil
Salt to taste

For masala powder
1½ tbsp coriander *(dhania)* seeds
 6 nos. cloves *(laung)*
25 mm. (1") piece cinnamon *(dalchini)*
1 tbsp cumin seeds *(jeera)*

For the masala powder

Dry roast all the masala ingredients on a tawa, till you get the aroma. Cool and grind to fine powder. Keep aside.

How to proceed

1. Pressure cook the corn for two whistles. Drain and keep aside.
2. Purée the tomatoes in a blender with ¼ cup of water. Keep aside.
3. Blend the onions to a smooth paste in the blender.
4. Heat oil in a pan and sauté the onions until they turn light brown.
5. Add the tomatoes and sauté on medium flame till the oil separates from the mixture.
6. Add the masala powder, salt and red chilli powder and cook for some more time.
7. Add about 2 cups of water and the corn cobs. Simmer for 5 minutes on medium flame.

   Serve hot.

Kaju Kismis Curry

Pineapple gravy enriched with raisins and cashewnuts

Preparation time: 10 minutes.   Cooking time: 15 minutes.   Serves 2.

½ cup raisins *(kismis)*, soaked in lukewarm water for 20 minutes
¼ cup broken cashew *(kaju)*
25 mm. (1") piece cinnamon *(dalchini)*
2 cloves *(laung)*
2 cardamon *(elaichi)*
1 tsp cumin seeds *(jeera)*
2 tbsp tomato ketchup
a pinch turmeric powder *(haldi)*
½ tsp red chilli powder
¾ cup milk
2 tsp sugar
2 tbsp chopped coriander
2 tbsp oil
Salt as per taste

To be ground into a paste
2 tbsp broken cashewnuts *(kaju)*
1 green chilli
1 cup chopped pineapple *(ananas)*

1. Heat the oil in a pan and add cinnamon, cloves, cardamon and cumin seeds.
2. When they crackle add in the paste and sauté till it leave oil from the sides.
3. Add in the tomato sauce, turmeric powder, red chilli powder, salt and sugar.
4. Add the cashew pieces, ½ cup water and milk and bring to a boil.
5. While serving, heat the gravy again and add the soaked raisins and garnish with coriander.

VARIATION: Kaju Grapes Curry

Use fresh green grapes instead of raisins for the above recipe.

International Curries

⌣ Vietnamese Curry ⌣

Picture on facing page.

Vegetarian version of the usually chicken-based curry that I tasted on a trip to Vietnam

Preparation time: 15 minutes.   Cooking time: 10 minutes.   Serves 4.

1 cup potato chunks
½ cup lemon grass *(hare chai ki patti)*
1 cup sliced onions
1 tbsp chopped ginger-garlic
2 bay leaves *(tej patta)*
½ tsp turmeric powder *(haldi)*
½ cup chopped tomatoes
½ cup cubed carrots

VIETNAMESE CURRY : Recipe above. ⇢

1 tbsp curry powder
1½ cup coconut milk
1 tsp cornflour
½ cup broccoli florets
½ cup tofu cubes
1 tsp sugar
1 tbsp chopped coriander
Salt to taste

1. Blend lemon grass with ¼ cup water. Strain and keep the water aside.
2. Dissolve the cornflour in the coconut milk. Keep aside.
3. Mix potatoes, onions, ginger-garlic, bay leaves and two cups of water and put to boil.
4. When potatoes are half cooked, add turmeric powder, tomatoes and carrots.
5. Add lemon grass water, salt, curry powder and bring to a boil.
6. Add coconut milk, broccoli and tofu and simmer for two minutes.
7. Add sugar if required.
   Serve hot garnished with chopped coriander.

Handy Tip: To make a substitute for curry powder, combine 1 tbsp of coriander cumin seed *(dhania-jeera)* powder with 2 pinches of sambar powder and add to this recipe.

~ Ceylonese Curry ~

A sure hit at any party. I recommend using readymade coconut milk in this recipe

Preparation time: 30 minutes.   Cooking time: 15 minutes.   Serves 4.

For the ceylonese curry
2 large coconuts
1 cup chopped mixed vegetables (carrots, french beans, green peas)
¼ tsp turmeric *(haldi)* powder
3 tsp coriander-cumin seed *(dhania-jeera)* powder
2 tsp red chilli powder
1½ cup chopped onions
4 curry leaves *(kadi patta)*
2 slit green chillies
5 peppercorns
3 small sticks cinnamon *(dalchini)*
½ tsp fenugreek *(methi)* seeds
1 cup boiled and cubed potatoes
1½ cup chopped tomatoes

Salt to taste

To be ground into Sambol chutney (For serving)
½ no. freshly grated coconut
½ cup chopped onion
1 tsp red chilli powder
1 tsp lemon juice
Salt to taste

To serve
2 to 3 cups boiled rice or noodles

1. Grate the coconut. Add 5 cups of water and blend in a liquidiser. Strain and take out the coconut milk. Keep aside.
2. To the coconut milk, add the mixed vegetables, turmeric powder, coriander-cumin seed powder, chilli powder, onions, curry leaves, green chilllies, peppercorns, cinnamon, fenugreek seeds and salt.
3. Cook until the vegetables are tender. Add the potatoes and tomatoes and boil for little minutes more.
   Serve hot with sambol chutney and boiled rice or noodles.

Handy Tip : You can use milk powder packets if fresh coconut is not available.

~ Thai Red Curry ~

A traditional fiery red Thai curry simmered with assorted vegetables.
An excellent complement to steamed rice

Preparation time: 10 minutes.   Cooking time: 15 minutes.   Serves 4 to 6.

6 to 7 tbsp red curry paste, recipe below
2 cups coconut milk
1 tbsp cornflour
½ tsp soya sauce
15 chopped basil leaves
½ cup diced baby corn
2 diced brinjals
1 cup broccoli florets
½ cup sliced mushrooms
1 tbsp oil
Salt to taste

For the red curry paste

5 red chilles, soaked in warm water for 10 minutes and drained
½ cup chopped onions
2 cloves garlic, peeled
2 teaspoons grated ginger
2 stalks lemon grass *(hare chai ki patti)*
6 stalks coriander
2 tsps coriander *(dhania)* powder
1 tbsp cumin seed *(jeera)* powder
2 tsp pepper powder
Salt to taste

For the red curry paste

1. Grind all the ingredients to a paste in a mortar or a food processor using a little water.
2. Store in an airtight container (for upto 1 month). Alternatively, freeze for upto 3 months. Keep aside.

How to proceed

1. Mix the cornflour and coconut milk
2. Heat the oil in a large pan; add the red curry paste and fry for a few minutes.

3. Add the coconut milk, soya sauce, basil leaves and all the vegetables.
4. Simmer for 10 minutes till the vegetables are tender.
5. Add salt.
6. Boil for 1 to 2 minutes till the curry thickens
   Serve hot with steamed rice or noodles.

Handy tip : Coconut milk is readliy available in tetrapacks but it can also be made at home by blending freshly grated coconut with water and then straining the mixture.

Kadhis

Gujarati Kadhi

The queen of all kadhis. This is my mothers recipe. Remember to use very fresh curds for this recipe

Preparation time: a few minutes.   Cooking time: 15 minutes.   Serves 4.

2 tbsp *besan* (Bengal gram flour)
2 cups beaten fresh curds *(dahi)*
1 tsp green chilli-ginger paste
2 curry leaves *(kadi patta)*
2 tbsp sugar
Salt to taste

For the tempering
½ tsp cumin *(jeera)* seeds

½ tsp mustard (*rai*) seeds
A pinch asafoetida (*hing*)
1 whole dry red chilli, broken into pieces
1 tsp oil
1 tsp ghee

For the garnish
2 tbsp chopped coriander

1. Whisk the *besan* and curds together till smooth and free of lumps.
2. Add the green chilli-ginger paste, curry leaves, sugar, salt and 2 cups of water and put to boil.
3. After it comes to a boil, lower the flame and simmer for a few minutes while stiring continuously.
4. Prepare the tempering by heating the oil and ghee and frying the cumin seeds and mustard seeds until they crackle. Add the asafoetida and red chilli.
5. Add this tempering to the kadhi and simmer for a few more minutes.
   Serve hot garnished with coriander.

Sindhi Kadhi

Picture on facing page.

One of my versions of the Sindhi Kadhi

Preparation time: 10 minutes. Cooking time: 20 minutes. Serves 4.

¼ cup cluster beans *(gavarfali)*
½ cup peeled and sliced potato
¼ cup peeled and sliced carrots
¼ cup lady finger *(bhindi)*, slit into two
½ tsp cumin seeds *(jeera)*
½ tsp fenugreek *(methi)* seeds
¼ tsp asafoetida *(hing)*
4 tbsp *besan* (Bengal gram flour)
2 tsp chopped green chillies
1 tsp grated ginger
4 to 6 curry leaves *(kadi patta)*
¼ tsp turmeric powder *(haldi)*
2 tsp red chilli powder

SINDHI KADHI : Recipe above. →

1 to 2 tbsp tamarind *(imli)* pulp
3 tbsp oil
Salt to taste

1. Boil the cluster beans, potato and carrots in 2 cups of water till they are tender. Keep aside, retaining the water.
2. Heat the oil in another pan and add the cumin seeds and fenugreek seeds. When they crackle add the asafoetida.
3. Add the *besan* and sauté for 4 to 5 minutes over a medium flame till it is golden brown in colour.
4. Add 3 cups of water, beat well and bring to a boil.
5. Add the green chillies, ginger, curry leaves, turmeric powder, chilli powder, tamarind pulp, all the cooked vegetables along with the water, lady finger and salt and bring to a boil. Simmer till the lady fingers is cooked.
   Serve hot with rice.

∽ Bhatia Kadhi ↶

A sweet and sour kadhi made with toovar dal liquid, curds and vegetables

Preparation time: 30 minutes.   Cooking time: 20 minutes.   Serves 4.

½ cup toovar *(arhar dal)*
¼ cup fresh curds *(dahi)*, beaten
1 tbsp *besan* (Bengal gram flour)
3 to 4 kokum, soaked in water
4 tbsp jaggery *(gur)*
1 cup lady finger *(bhindi)*, cut into 50 mm. (2") pieces
½ cup sliced radish *(mooli)*
4 to 6 drumsticks *(saijan ki phalli saragavo)*, cut into 50 mm. (2") pieces
½ cup thickly sliced firm ripe bananas
Salt to taste

For the tempering
1 tsp cumin seeds *(jeera)*

½ tsp mustard seeds *(rai)*
¼ tsp asafoetida *(hing)*
½ tsp fenugreek *(methi)* seeds
2 tbsp oil

For the garnish
2 tbsp chopped coriander

1. Wash and pressure-cook the toovar dal in 5 to 6 cups of water.
2. Cool and strain out the dal. Keep it aside to make any dal. You will need only the liquid for this recipe.
3. Combine the curds and besan till the mixture is smooth and free of lumps. Keep aside.
4. Prepare the tempering by heating the oil in a saucepan adding the cumin seeds, mustard seeds, asafoetida and fenugreek seeds and frying till the seeds crackle.
5. Add the lady finger, radish, drumsticks, the strained dal liquid and salt and simmer till the vegetables are cooked.
6. Add the kokum, jaggery and the curds-besan mixture and mix well till smooth.
7. Add the banana slices and simmer for 15 minutes.
   Serve hot garnished with coriander.

Punjabi Kadhi

A curry with crunchy fried pakodis and a mouth-watering tempering

Preparation time: 15 minutes.   Cooking time: 30 minutes.   Serves 4.

For the pakodis
1 cup *besan* (Bengal gram flour)
2 tbsp chopped coriander
¼ tsp turmeric powder *(haldi)*
A pinch soda bi-carb
1 tsp cumin seeds *(jeera)*
1 tsp finely chopped green chillies
Salt to taste
Oil for deep-frying

For the kadhi
2 cups beaten fresh curds *(dahi)*
2 tbsp *besan* (Bengal gram flour)

¼ tsp turmeric *(haldi)* powder
Salt to taste

For the tempering
12 mm. (½") stick cinnamon *(dalchini)*
2 cloves *(laung)*
2 whole dry red chillies
½ tsp coriander *(dhania)* seeds
½ tsp cumin seeds *(jeera)*
¼ tsp fenugreek *(methi)* seeds
2 tsp grated ginger
4 to 6 curry leaves *(kadi patta)*
½ tsp red chilli powder
2 tbsp oil

For the pakodis
1. Mix all the ingredients for the pakodis except the oil and add a little water to make a thick batter.
2. Heat the oil in a kadhai and drop spoonfuls of the batter into the hot oil.
3. Deep-fry till the pakodis are crisp and golden brown. Drain on absorbent paper. Keep aside.

For the kadhi

1. Mix the curds, *besan*, turmeric powder and salt with 2 cups of water till smooth and free of lumps.
2. Bring to a boil.
3. Heat the oil in a pan and fry the tempering ingredients for 2 minutes. Keep aside.
4. Pour the tempering over the kadhi, lower the flame and simmer for 10 to 12 minutes. Keep aside.

How to proceed

1. Re-heat the kadhi and bring to a boil, lower the flame.
2. Drop the pakodis into the simmering kadhi and cook for a few minutes. Serve hot.

Handy tips : 1. When you add the pakodis into the kadhi, add one first and check again to see that it does not crumble or disintegrate.
2. If that happens, add some more besan to the pakodi mixture and check.

Pakoda Kadhi

Delicious palak pakodas soaked in tangy kadhi

Preparation time: 15 minutes.   Cooking time: 20 minutes.   Serves 4.

For the *palak* pakodas
1 cup blanched, drained and chopped
spinach *(palak)*
¼ cup *besan* (Bengal gram flour)
½ tsp chilli powder
½ tsp cumin seeds *(jeera)*
A pinch soda bi-carbonate
Salt to taste
Oil for deep-frying

For the kadhi
1 cup curds *(dahi)*
2 tbsp *besan* (Bengal gram flour)
1 tsp cumin seeds *(jeera)*
A pinch asafoetida *(hing)*
5 curry leaves *(kadi patta)*
½ cup sliced onions
1 tsp finely chopped garlic
¼ tsp turmeric powder *(haldi)*
1 tbsp oil
Salt to taste

For the *palak* pakodas
1. Mix the spinach leaves, besan, chilli powder, cumin seeds, soda bi-carb and salt
   with enough water in a bowl to make a soft dough.

2. Divide into 8 equal portions and shape into even-sized rounds.
3. Heat the oil in a kadai and deep-fry the pakodas over a medium flame till they are golden brown.
4. Remove and drain on absorbent paper. Keep aside.

For the kadhi
1. Beat the curds and besan till smooth and free of lumps. Keep aside.
2. Heat the oil in a pan and add the cumin seeds. When they crackle, add the asafoetida, curry leaves, onions and garlic and sauté for 4 to 5 minutes.
3. Add the curds and *besan* mixture, turmeric powder, salt and 2 cups of water and bring to a boil whilst stirring continuously.

How to proceed
Just before serving, add the palak pakodas to the hot kadhi and simmer for 4 to 5 minutes.
Serve hot with rice.

ᷔ Gatte ki Kadhi ᷔ

Picture on facing page.

Rajasthani preparation of gram flour dumplings in a rich yoghurt gravy served with Basmati rice

Preparation time: 20 minutes.   Cooking time: 25 minutes.   Serves 4.

For the gattas
¾ cup *besan* (Bengal gram flour)
1 tsp chilli powder
1 tsp fennel seeds *(saunf)*
a pinch *ajwain* (carom seeds)
1 tbsp curds *(dahi)*
2 tbsp oil
Salt to taste

For the kadhi
2 cups fresh curds *(dahi)*
2 tbsp *besan* (Bengal gram flour)
4 to 6 curry leaves *(kadi patta)*

GATTE KI KADHI: Recipe above. ➔

1 tsp cumin seeds *(jeera)*
½ tsp mustard seeds *(rai)*
½ tsp fennel seeds *(saunf)*
¼ tsp asafoetida *(hing)*
1 bay leaf *(tej patta)*
1 clove *(laung)*
1 stick cinnamon *(dalchini)*
1 cardamom *(elaichi)*
¼ tsp turmeric powder *(haldi)*
2 tsp red chilli powder
2 tsp coriander *(dhania)* powder
2 tbsp chopped coriander
2 tbsp oil
Salt to taste

For the gattas
1. Combine all the ingredients for the gattas. Knead into a firm dough using 1 to 2 tbsp of water.
2. Divide the mixture into 8 equal portions and shape each portion into a 75 mm. (3") long cylindrical roll.
3. Boil plenty of water in a pan and cook the gattas in boiling water for 7 to 8 minutes.

Drain and disacrd the water.
4. Cool and cut the gattas into 12 mm. (½") long pieces. Keep aside.

For the kadhi
1. Combine the curds, *besan*, ½ cup of water and curry leaves and beat well to get a smoth mixture that is free of lumps. Keep aside.
2. Heat the oil in a pan; add the cumin seeds, mustard seeds, fennel seeds, asafoetida, bay leaf, clove, cinnamon and cardamom.
3. When the seeds crackle, add the turmeric powder, chilli powder and coriander powder and sauté for a few seconds.
4. Add the curd mixture, 1½ cups of water and salt and bring to a boil while stirring continuously, so that the kadhi does not split. Keep aside.

How to proceed
Add the prepared gattas to the kadhi and simmer for a few minutes.
Garnish with coriander and serve hot.

Chana Kofta Kadhi

Unusual koftas made from chick peas served with the traditional kadhi

Preparation time: 15 minutes.   Cooking time: 20 minutes.   Serves 4.

For the kadhi
2 cups fresh curds *(dahi)*
1 tbsp *besan* (Bengal gram flour)
½ tsp finely chopped green chilles
1 tsp grated ginger
½ tbsp grated garlic
¼ tsp turmeric powder *(haldi)*
½ tsp cumin seeds *(jeera)*
1 stick cinnamon *(dalchini)*
¼ tsp asafoetida *(hing)*
1 tbsp oil
Salt to taste

For the chana koftas
⅓ cup *kabuli chana* (chick peas), soaked
overnight and boiled
½ cup chopped coriander
½ cup chopped mint *(phudina)*
¼ cup chopped parsley
½ tsp chopped green chillies
Salt to taste

For the chana koftas
1. Drain the cooked kabuli chana.
2. Grind all the ingredients to a fine paste in a blender without using water.
3. Divide the mixture into 40 equal portions and shape each portion into an even sized round. Keep aside.

For the kadhi
1. Combine the curds, *besan* and turmeric powder with ½ cup of water and mix well. Keep aside.
2. Make a paste out of green chilli, ginger and garlic. Keep aside.
3. Heat the oil in a pan and add the cumin seeds, cinnamon and asafoetida.
4. When the cumin seeds crackle, add the curds and besan mixture, prepared green chilli paste, salt and 1 cup of water and simmer for 5 to 10 minutes. Keep aside.

How to proceed
1. Re-heat the kadhi and bring it to a boil. Lower the flame.
2. Drop the prepared koftas in the simmering kadhi and cook for about 10 minutes. Serve hot.

Handy tip: If the kofta mixture is difficult to shape into rounds, you may need to add 1 tbsp *besan* (Bengal gram flour) to the mixture and mix well.

Dapka Kadhi

Picture on cover.

Moong dal dumplings cooked in a traditional Gujarati Kadhi

Preparation time: 15 minutes.   Cooking time: 15 minutes.   Serves 4 to 6.

For the dapkas
1 cup yellow *moong dal* (split yellow gram)
1 tbsp oil
1 tsp green chilli-ginger paste
½ tsp sugar
A pinch soda-bi-carb
Salt to taste

For the kadhi
2 cups fresh curds *(dahi)*
2 tbsp *besan* Bengal gram flour
1 tsp green chilli-ginger paste
2 curry leaves *(kadi patta)*

2 tsp sugar
½ tsp cumin seeds *(jeera)*
½ tsp mustard seeds *(rai)*
A pinch asafoetida *(hing)*
1 whole dry red chilli, broken into pieces
2 tbsp chopped coriadner
2 tsp oil
Salt to taste

For the dapkas
1. Soak the moong dal in lukewarm for 3 to 4 hours. Drain.
2. Grind the soaked moong dal to a fine paste in a blender without adding water.
3. Add the oil, green chilli-ginger paste, sugar, soda bi-carb and salt and mix well. Keep aside.

For the kadhi
1. Beat the *besan*, curds and ½ cup of water till smooth and free of lumps.
2. Add the green chilli-ginger paste, curry leaves, sugar, salt and 2 cups of water and put to boil.
3. Simmer for a while whilst stirring occasionally.

4. Prepare the tempering by heating the oil and frying the cumin and mustard seeds until they crackle. Add the asafoetida and red chilli.
5. Add the tempering to the kadhi and boil for a few minutes.

How to proceed
1. Remove the boiling kadhi from the flame and add in the dapka batter a little at a time using your fingertips to form dumplings and keep aside for about 10 minutes till the dapkas float.
2. Simmer for 5 to 7 minutes.
3. Sprinkle coriander on top and serve hot.

Handy tips: 1. First add one dapka and wait for it to float up. If it does not float, this means the batter is too thin.
2. Add a little gram flour to the dapka batter and try again.

Tamater ki Kadhi

A simple tomato based curry

Preparation time: 10 minutes.   Cooking time: 30 minutes.   Serves 4.

4 large tomatoes
½ tsp mustard seeds *(rai)*
½ tsp cumin *(jeera)* seeds
1 chopped green chilli
5 to 6 curry leaves *(kadi patta)*
2 cloves *(laung)*
2 tbsp *besan* (Bengal gram flour)
¼ tsp turmeric powder *(haldi)*
2 tsp red chilli powder
A pinch asafoetida *(hing)*
2 tbsp grated jaggery *(gur)*
2 tbsp chopped coriander
2 tbsp oil
Salt to taste

1. Roughly chop the tomatoes and cook them with ½ cup of water for about 10 to 15 minutes.
2. Cool and blend in a food processor to a get a smooth purée. Keep aside.
3. Heat the oil in a saucepan and add the mustard seeds and cumin seeds. When they crackle, add the green chillies, curry leaves, cloves and *besan* and cook for 2 to 3 minutes.
4. Add the turmeric, red chilli powder, asafoetida and puréed tomatoes with 2 cups of water and cook on a medium flame, stirring continuously.
5. When the kadhi comes to a boil, add the jaggery and salt and simmer for another 5 minutes.
6. Remove from the fire.
   Garnish with coriander and serve hot with rice.

Soya Mutter ki Kadhi

Soyabean nuggets and peas simmered in a tangy curd based gravy

Preparation time: 10 minutes.   Cooking time: 40 minutes.   Serves 4.

¼ cup soya nuggets
½ cup green peas
½ tsp cumin seeds *(jeera)*
A pinch asafoetida *(hing)*
1 tsp green chilli-ginger paste
½ tsp garlic paste
½ cup chopped onions
½ cup finely chopped tomatoes
¼ tsp turmeric powder *(haldi)*
½ tsp red chilli powder
½ tsp coriander *(dhania)* powder
1½ cups fresh curds *(dahi)*
2 tbsp *besan* (Bengal gram flour)
3 tbsp milk

½ tsp sugar
2 tbsp chopped coriander
2 tbsp oil
Salt to taste

1. Cook the soya nuggets in hot salted water for about 20 minutes. Keep aside.
2. Heat the oil in a pan and add the cumin seeds. When they crackle, add the asafoetida, green chilli-ginger, garlic paste and onions and saute till the onions are translucent.
3. Add the tomatoes, turmeric powder, chilli powder and coriander powder and cook on a slow flame for about 5 to 10 minutes.
4. Meanwhile beat the curds, *besan*, milk and ½ cup of water till smooth and free of lumps. Add to the onion-tomato gravy.
5. Add the soya nuggets, green peas, sugar, salt and 1½ cups of water and bring to a boil.
   Serve hot garnished with coriander.

⋄ Dahi Chane ki Kadhi ⋄

A pulse enriched kadhi

Preparation time: 15 minutes.   Cooking time: 15 minutes.   Serves 4.

1 cup red chana (whole red gram), soaked overnight and drained
½ tsp cumin seeds *(jeera)*
¼ tsp mustard seeds *(rai)*
2 bay leaves *(tej patta)*
4 whole red chillies, broken into pieces
1/8 tsp asafoetida *(hing)*
2 tsp green chilli-ginger paste
1 tsp red chilli powder
¼ tsp turmeric powder *(haldi)*
2 cups fresh curds *(dahi)*
4 tsp *besan* (Bengal gram flour)
2 tbsp chopped coriander
1 tbsp oil
Salt to taste

1. Heat the oil in a pressure cooker and add the cumin seeds, mustard seeds, bay leaves, red chillies and asafoetida.
2. When the seeds crackle, add the red chana, green chilli-ginger, chilli powder, turmeric powder, salt and 2 cups of water. Pressure cook for 2 to 3 whistles till the chana is cooked.
3. Beat the curds and *besan* together. Add this curd mixture and ½ cup of water to the cooked chana and bring to a boil while stirring continuously. Simmer for 4 to 5 minutes.
   Serve hot garnished with coriander.

❧ Kokum Kadhi ❧

Also called sol kadhi, this tangy kadhi is had cold with luke warm rice or even consumed like an appetizing drink

Preparation time: 10 minutes.   Cooking time: 2 minutes.   Serves 4.

10 to 12 semi dried kokum
2 cups freshly grated coconut
2 tsp crushed green chillies
2 tbsp chopped coriander
Salt to taste

For the tempering
1 whole dry red chilli, broken into pieces
1 tsp cumin seeds *(jeera)*
A pinch asafoetida *(hing)*
2 to 4 curry leaves *(kadi patta)*
2 tsp oil

1. Soak the kokum, salt and green chillies in ¼ cup of water and keep aside for 15 to 20 minutes.
2. Strain and squeeze out the kokum and green chillies, retaining the water.
3. Blend the coconut, green chilli and ½ cup of water for about one minute.
4. Strain through a muslin cloth.
5. Keep the coconut milk aside and blend the residue again with ½ cup of water.
6. Strain again.
7. Add the kokum water to the coconut milk. Keep aside.
8. Heat oil in a pan, add in cumin seeds,when they crackle add the curry leaves.
9. Add in the asafoetida and red chillies. Pour this tempering over the coconut milk mixture.

    Garnish with coriander and serve cold with luke warm rice.

Coconut Kadhi

My favourite kadhi. Coconut milk is now available in tetrapacks at grocery stores, so you need not go through the effort of extracting it!

Preparation time: 40 minutes.   Cooking time: 30 minutes.   Serves 6.

1½ cups coconut milk
2 tbsp *besan* (Bengal gram flour)
¾ cup fresh curds *(dahi)*
2 cardamom *(elaichi)*
2 cloves *(laung)*
25 mm. (1") stick cinnamon *(dalchini)*
1 bay leaf *(tej patta)*
6 curry leaves *(kadi patta)*
1 tsp grated ginger
½ tsp chopped green chillies
2 tsp oil
Salt to taste

1. Add the *besan* to the curds beat well and keep aside.
2. Heat the oil in a pan and add the cardamom, cloves, cinnamon, bay leaf and curry leaves.
3. When the curry leaves splutter, add the ginger and green chilli and stir for a few seconds.
4. Add the coconut milk and 1 cup of water and bring to a boil, while stirring continuously.
5. Add the besan-curds mixture and salt and mix well. Simmer on a slow flame till the kadhi thickens while stirring constantly.
   Serve hot garnished with coriander.

Mini Series by *Tarla Dalal*

Healthy Breakfast

Healthy Snacks

Healthy
Soups & Salads

Healthy Juices

Fast Foods
Made Healthy

Calcium
Rich Recipes

Iron Rich Recipes

Forever Young Diet

Home Remedies

Low Cholesterol
Recipes